Level 2.0

0.5

D1270610

OCEANS ALIVE

Sea Shells

by Shari Skeie

BELLWETHER MEDIA • MINNEAPOLIS, MN

Note to Librarians, Teachers, and Parents:

Blastoff! Readers are carefully developed by literacy experts and combine standards-based content with developmentally appropriate text.

Level 1 provides the most support through repetition of high-frequency words, light text, predictable sentence patterns, and strong visual support.

Level 2 offers early readers a bit more challenge through varied simple sentences, increased text load, and less repetition of high-frequency words.

Level 3 advances early-fluent readers toward fluency through increased text and concept load, less reliance on visuals, longer sentences, and more literary language.

Level 4 builds reading stamina by providing more text per page, increased use of punctuation, greater variation in sentence patterns, and increasingly challenging vocabulary.

Level 5 encourages children to move from "learning to read" to "reading to learn" by providing even more text, varied writing styles, and less familiar topics.

Whichever book is right for your reader, Blastoff! Readers are the perfect books to build confidence and encourage a love of reading that will last a lifetime!

This edition first published in 2009 by Bellwether Media.

No part of this publication may be reproduced in whole or in part without written permission of the publisher. For information regarding permission, write to Bellwether Media Inc., Attention: Permissions Department, Post Office Box 19349, Minneapolis, MN 55419.

Library of Congress Cataloging-in-Publication Data
Skeie, Shari.
  Sea shells / by Shari Skeie.
    p. cm. — (Blastoff! readers. Oceans alive)
  Summary: "Simple text and full color photographs introduce beginning readers to sea shells. Developed by literacy experts for students in kindergarten through third grade"—Provided by publisher.
  Includes bibliographical references and index.
  ISBN-13: 978-1-60014-208-6 (hardcover : alk. paper)
  ISBN-10: 1-60014-208-7 (hardcover : alk. paper)
  1. Shells—Juvenile literature. I. Title.
  QL405.2.S57 2009
  594.147'7—dc22
                                          2008017350

Contents

Sea shells are the hard, outside **skeleton** of some sea animals.

4

The hard shell is called an **exoskeleton**. It protects the animal's soft body.

5

The shell is made mostly of **calcium**. Calcium makes up our bones too.

Most animals make shells from calcium in the water. Shells grow as the animal gets bigger.

The lines on this shell form a spiral shape. Sea shells that form spirals are called **univalves**.

8

murex shell

moon snail shells

worm shell

Moon snail, murex, worm, and conch shells are univalves.

Moon snail shells have a spiral pattern that looks like an eye.

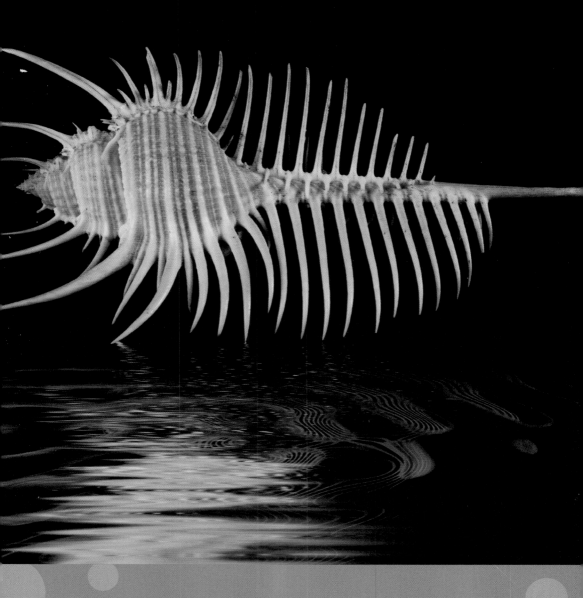

Murex shells have **spines**.
This shell looks like a comb.

A worm shell is a long, thin spiral. It is hollow like a straw.

A conch shell has a pink
inside. The outside is dull
and bumpy.

Some sea shells have two matching parts. These are called **bivalves**.

Oyster, scallop, and coquina shells are bivalves.

Oyster shells are rough
on the outside. The inside
is shiny.

Scallop shells can be
many different colors.
They have ridges.

Coquina shells have
striped patterns.

Some animals don't make their own shells. They may use an empty shell.

19

This hermit crab found
a shell that fits.

The hermit crab will grow.
Some day it will need a
bigger shell!

21

Glossary

bivalves—sea shells with two matching parts

calcium—the mineral that makes up most of a sea shell

exoskeleton—a bony structure on the outside of an animal; sea shells are the exoskeletons of some sea animals.

skeleton—a hard structure that supports and protects the body

spines—hard and sharp parts of a plant or animal

univalves—sea shells that grow in a spiral shape

To Learn More

AT THE LIBRARY

Berkes, Marianne. *Seashells by the Seashore*. Nevada City, Calif.: Dawn Publications, 2002.

Tibbitts, Christiane Kump. *Seashells, Crabs, & Sea Stars*. Minnetonka, Minn.: NorthWord Books for Young Readers, 1998.

Wallace, Nancy Elizabeth. *Shells! Shells! Shells!* Tarrytown, NY: Marshall Cavendish, 2007.

ON THE WEB

Learning more about sea shells is as easy as 1, 2, 3.

1. Go to www.factsurfer.com

2. Enter "sea shells" into search box.

3. Click the "Surf" button and you will see a list of related web sites.

With factsurfer.com, finding more information is just a click away.

Index

The images in this book are reproduced through the courtesy of: Danabeth555, front cover; ImageState / Alamy, pp. 4-5; Tatiana Grozetskaya, p. 6; Brandon Cole Marine Photography / Alamy, p. 7; David Fleetham / Getty Images, p. 8; Linnea Vogelzang-Brown, pp. 9, 10, 12; Bershadsky Yuri, p. 9; Eremin Sergey, p. 11; Mitch Diamond / Alamy, p. 13; Alex James Bramwell, p. 14; Ian Nolan / Alamy, p. 15; LOOK Die Bildagentur der Fotografen GmbH / Alamy, p. 16 (inset); Niall McDiarmid / Alamy, p. 16; Clark Wheeler, p. 17; tbkmedia.de / Alamy, p. 18; Marevision / Masterfile, p. 19; Paul Nicklin / Getty Images, pp. 20-21.